HOW?D THEY DO THAT?

in...

ANCIENT ROME

Mitchell Lane
PUBLISHERS

P.O. Box 196
Hockessin, Delaware 19707

HOW?D THEY DO THAT? *in...*

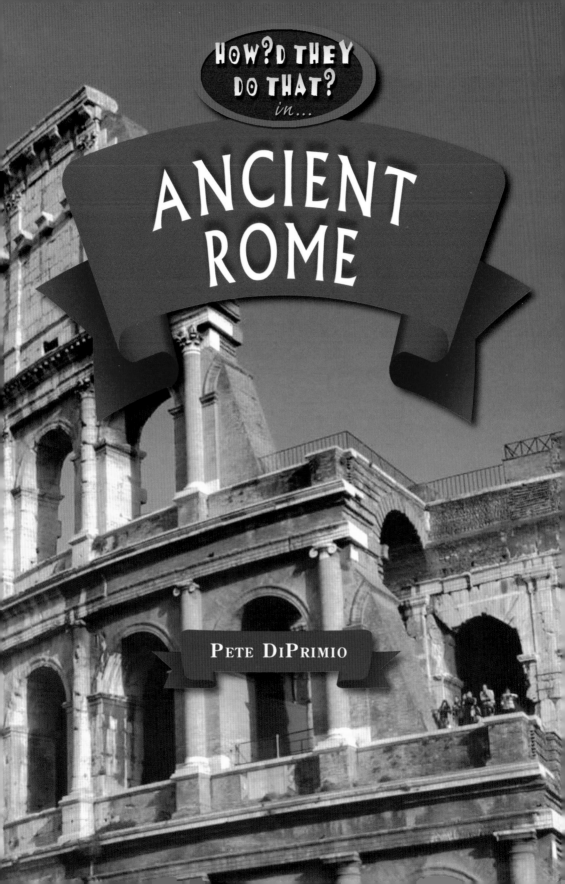

HOW?D THEY DO THAT?

in...

ANCIENT ROME

PETE DiPrimio

Copyright © 2010 by Mitchell Lane Publishers, Inc. All rights reserved. No part
of this book may be reproduced without written permission from the publisher.
Printed and bound in the United States of America.

Printing   1   2   3   4   5   6   7   8   9

Library of Congress Cataloging-in-Publication Data
DiPrimio, Pete.
  How'd they do that in ancient Rome / by Pete DiPrimio.
        p. cm.—(How'd they do that)
  Includes bibliographical references and index.
  ISBN 978-1-58415-820-2 (library bound)
  1. Rome—History—Juvenile literature. 2. Rome—Social life and customs—Juvenile
literature.   I. Title.
  DG77.D594 2010
  937—dc22

                                                                    2009027342

AUTHOR'S NOTE: The mark SPQR stands for *Senatus Populusque Romanus,* which
can be translated as "The Senate and People of Rome" or "The Roman Senate and
the People." It was the mark of the Roman Republic.

PUBLISHER'S NOTE: This story is based on the author's extensive research, which
he believes to be accurate. Documentation of his research is on page 60.

     To reflect current usage, we have chosen to use the secular era designations
BCE ("before the common era") and CE ("of the common era") instead of the
traditional designations BC ("before Christ") and AD (*anno Domini,* "in the year of
the Lord").

     The internet sites referenced herein were active as of the publication date. Due
to the fleeting nature of some web sites, we cannot guarantee they will all be active
when you are reading this book.

CONTENTS

INTRODUCTION

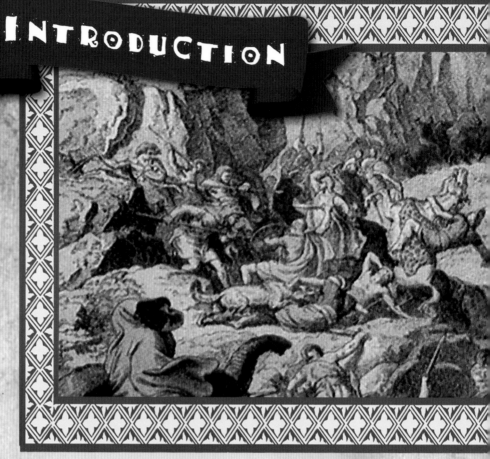

Maximus paced in the brightening dawn. His stomach rumbled, but he refused to eat. His body screamed for sleep, but his mind raced too fast for that to happen.

Hannibal was coming. So were elephants. So was war.

Was Maximus ready for this?

Maximus was eighteen years old and a Roman soldier, or legionnaire, stationed in what is now northwestern Italy. He had never fought in a battle before. He had never faced death before. That was about to change.

It was 218 BCE (Before the Common Era) and Hannibal, a general from the Mediterranean city-state of Carthage, was bringing war to the Romans. Carthage was a long-established power. Rome was an up-and-coming challenger. In the Mediterranean, there was room for just one superpower. Would it be Carthage or Rome?

Rome had beaten Carthage in the first of the Punic Wars twenty-three years earlier, and Carthage wanted revenge. The first war had

been fought at sea. This one would be fought in Italy, because Hannibal wanted the Roman people and leaders to feel his anger. He believed it would be the best way to restore Carthage to power. Now he was leading his army from Spain and across Gaul (now France) to threaten the Roman way of life.

Maximus was determined to do his part to stop Hannibal. His family, which owned a farm on the plains around Rome, was right in Hannibal's path. Maximus joined the army even though his mother had begged him not to. His father understood. His younger sisters pretended to understand.

Maximus had dark hair, olive skin, and eyes so blue girls teased him that looking into them was like looking at a piece of the sky. He was 5-foot-8 and 160 pounds, the size of most of the soldiers. He had just finished his legionnaire training, and his whole body was sore. His feet had blisters on blisters from nonstop marching. His shoulders ached from cuts and bruises and from carrying nearly 100 pounds of gear. He had survived drills so real that some soldiers' bones had been broken and blood had been spilled. Romans thrived on toughness. They believed their army was better than those they fought because they were so well disciplined and well trained. Their full-time soldiers enlisted for years—not like other powers, whose soldiers trained for part of the year but were farmers the rest of the time.

Maximus loved the army. He wanted to be a great legionnaire. He wanted to show how brave and strong he was. He couldn't stand the waiting. That was the worst part about being a soldier. Some might call it fear of the unknown, but Maximus wasn't afraid. He was eager to test himself, to defend his country and bring glory to his family.

Horsemen served as scouts and messengers.

Maximus had enlisted for twenty years. He got a yearly salary (112.5 Roman dollars, called *denarii*).[1] If he survived to retirement, he would get paid in land, although he knew it might not be the land he wanted, which was near his family's farm. He would worry about that later.

Dawn was coming and Maximus reached the edge of the camp. He thrust his throwing spear (called a pilum) into the dirt, leaned against it, and scanned the mountains in the distance, hoping to see a sign of the Carthaginians marching toward them. He carried a short Spanish sword (other soldiers used a longer Roman sword called a *gladius*) and a large wooden shield covered with leather and held together by iron. His body armor was a sleeveless coat of iron mail (overlapping iron scales) over a wool tunic. He had an iron helmet and wore leather sandals. All this could be heavy and hot during summer days, but Maximus didn't care. He was right where he wanted to be.

The eastern sky glowed on this cool early fall morning. Soon the sun would rise. Soldiers were waking. Campfires crackled all around

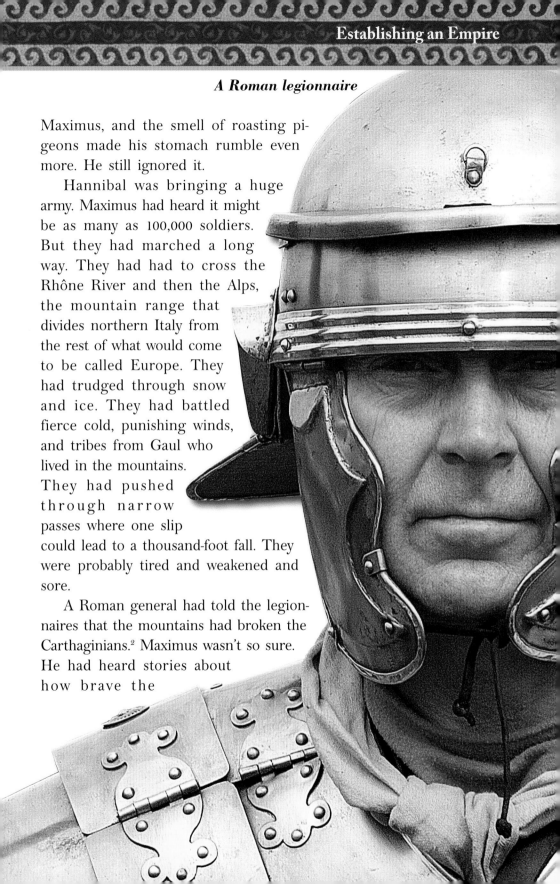

A Roman legionnaire

Maximus, and the smell of roasting pigeons made his stomach rumble even more. He still ignored it.

Hannibal was bringing a huge army. Maximus had heard it might be as many as 100,000 soldiers. But they had marched a long way. They had had to cross the Rhône River and then the Alps, the mountain range that divides northern Italy from the rest of what would come to be called Europe. They had trudged through snow and ice. They had battled fierce cold, punishing winds, and tribes from Gaul who lived in the mountains. They had pushed through narrow passes where one slip could lead to a thousand-foot fall. They were probably tired and weakened and sore.

A Roman general had told the legionnaires that the mountains had broken the Carthaginians.[2] Maximus wasn't so sure. He had heard stories about how brave the

Carthaginian soldiers were. They had the same armor and weapons as the Romans; the same drive to conquer and rule.

Maximus wanted them to be good fighters. He wanted them to be fierce, because then there would be more honor in defeating them. One thing he wasn't so sure about was the elephants. He had never seen them before, but he knew Hannibal was bringing them. How many? He didn't know. They were African elephants that could be as tall as 11 feet and weigh as much as 14,000 pounds. He knew they weren't meat eaters, so they wouldn't eat him. But they were very strong with very big feet that could stomp a soldier flat. They had long sharp ivory tusks that could rip through flesh. They could crush or scatter an army, which was why Hannibal was bringing them. Maximus knew Roman soldiers had faced elephants before and beaten them. Romans wouldn't scare and wouldn't scatter. They would be very disciplined, very aggressive, and very smart.

A fellow soldier shouted. Two legionnaires ran toward them, fast despite their gear. More soldiers shouted and pointed toward the north and the snow-capped mountains. Maximus squinted into the distance and there, moving in a bobbing wave, dust kicking up in its wake, was an advancing army.

Hannibal was here. So were the elephants. So was war.

Carthaginians and their elephants

Roman Warfare

Rome's empire was built on war and the success of its army. Romans conquered and then ruled, brutally if necessary. Roman expansion first began in 435 BCE when it attacked its Etruscan neighbors. At its peak, about 150 CE, the empire stretched from Great Britain and Spain through Central and Eastern Europe, to what is now the Middle East and all of North Africa. Romans never defeated the German tribes, who lived in a land of dark forests and swamps. Those same tribes were among the Barbarians who helped defeat the Roman Empire in 476 CE.

Rome became the main Mediterranean power after it defeated Carthage in three wars, called the Punic Wars, which were fought from 264 to 146 BCE. After the last war, Carthage was completely destroyed. Rome took charge of Eastern Europe by defeating the Greeks in a series of wars that ended in 133 BCE.

The great general Julius Caesar conquered the rich land of Gaul, which is now France. His army was famous for its quick strikes that helped him defeat the more numerous Gauls. The eight-year war ended in 50 BCE.

Roman military strategy was simple—it organized armies for many marches. Troops fought hard and fierce and fast. Generals were willing to lose a lot of soldiers to defeat enemies with larger armies.[3]

Fighting was basically hand to hand and was not only dangerous, but very tiring mentally and physically. Troops would take breaks, move a few yards away, and yell insults at each other before fighting again.

Sending troops to the frontiers took time. Even on the best of roads, troops with all their supplies could only go about 15 miles a day (30 miles with no supplies). It took 124 marching days, plus two days at sea, to travel from Rome to the city of Antioch, which was located in what is now Turkey.[4] The great distance, and the expense and difficulty in maintaining enough troops to defend the empire, eventually contributed to the fall of Rome.

Reenactors march as Roman legionnaires once did.

In The Colosseum, *an 1896 painting by Sir Lawrence Alma-Tadema, women watch from Roman rooftops as crowds head to the public games at the Colosseum.*

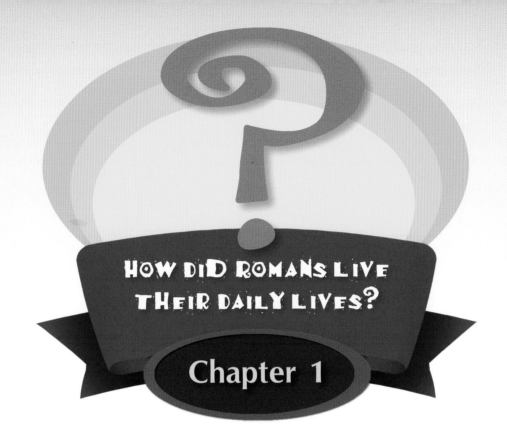

HOW DID ROMANS LIVE THEIR DAILY LIVES?

Chapter 1

What was it like to live in ancient Rome? Well, if you like a clean city, you'd have hated Rome. People threw their trash out the window and onto the streets. Not even daily sweeping of the main streets helped. At night, the city was crawling with criminals causing trouble. The poet Juvenal said it was stupid to go out at night without first having written a will.

There was a lot of action during the day. Shop owners displayed their goods on the streets to passing customers. There were so many people milling about that carts could not be driven on the streets.

The men generally got up before dawn to visit a public bathroom and catch up on all the news. Many of them would visit a patron, a rich man who often gave them money, then have lunch (usually bread and wine) and go to the public baths. Women would stay at home except when it was their turn to go to the public bath (they would go at a different time than the men).

Ancient Rome had a lot of slaves—about 400,000 in a population of 1 million. Rich people might own 500 slaves. Very rich people might own 4,000. Emperors owned as many as 20,000.[1]

Slaves did the building and the farming. They taught. They made pottery and jewelry and shoes. A non-slave could be a craftsman, such as a carpenter or a shopkeeper. Rich men could get into politics or law or join the army.

Many people didn't have a lot to do except go to the public games of gladiator fights and chariot races. The rich often vacationed in the resort towns of Pompeii and Herculaneum, which were on the lush west coast of Italy in the shadow of Mount Vesuvius.

PUBLIC BATHS

In ancient Rome, public baths were more about meeting people, talking to friends, and just hanging out than cleaning off dust and sweat. They were for everybody, from the very poor to the very rich. They didn't cost much to use. For those who wanted to relax, the baths had gardens with walking paths, libraries, barbershops, and restaurants. A person could also burn off stress the old-fashioned way—through exercise.

Most baths had a gymnasium or a training room where people could lift weights or play Roman ball or wrestle. They would go into a changing room and take off most of their clothes and all of their jewelry. Near the entrance was a security guard called a *capsarius* who would watch their stuff to make sure nobody stole it.

Romans believed staying fit and healthy was very important, and that included bathing in water of different temperatures. A person would start in the *laconicum,* a room with a pool filled with very hot water. Then he would go to the *tepidarium,* which had a warm-water pool. He'd end in the *frigidarium,* a room with a cold-water pool. Diving into the cold water would jolt his body, which was thought to be healthy. There was also a steam room called an *unctorium.* There, people would be covered with oil, which was used instead of soap. The next stop was the *sudatorium* (sauna), where they would scrape the sweat, dirt, and oil off their skin with a curved metal tool called a strigil. Finally, they'd have a relaxing massage and rest before going home.

SPQR

Roman baths are still around, though they are no longer used. One of the best preserved and most popular with tourists is this site in the British city of Bath.

When Mount Vesuvius erupted, it buried the coastal towns of Pompeii, Herculaneum, and Stabiae, killing thousands. The ash also preserved the towns. Painting: **Vesuvius Erupting at Night,** *William Marlow, 1768*

A Roman wouldn't do this in private. Other people would be there—some he knew, some he didn't. Either way, bathers would talk and find out what was—or wasn't—going on in the neighborhood, the city, the empire.

How did the Romans heat the water? They would make a tank of stone and raise it on brick pillars. Underneath, furnaces heated the water. Slaves would keep the fires in the furnaces going. The warm air from the fire would rise through the hollow walls and warm the room.[2]

During the reign of Augustus (27 BCE–14 CE), Rome had about 170 public baths. By 300 CE, there were around 900. Some were so big they could hold hundreds of people. The Baths of Caracalla, the largest bath in Rome, covered 33 acres and could hold 1,600 people. The oldest imperial bath, *Thermae Agrippae* (Agrippa's Bath), was named for the man who built it between 25 and 19 BCE. Marcus Agrippa was an equestrian gentleman (from the elite *equus,* or knightly, class) who was married to a daughter of Augustus Caesar, the emperor of Rome.

You can still visit Roman baths. Trajan's Bathhouse and the Baths of Caracalla still stand. There's also a well-preserved bathhouse in Pompeii, which was buried in volcanic ash when Mount Vesuvius erupted in 79 CE.

CLOTHING

People wore cotton tunics in the house and togas when they went out. A tunic was like a long, white shirt and was worn with a belt. Men wore short tunics with either no sleeves or short sleeves. Until late in the empire, only women wore tunics with long sleeves, called stolae. Men's tunics did not reach their ankles. Poor men wore a loincloth and a tunic. Tunics had different kinds of details sewn on them to show how important the people wearing them were, kind of like a rank in the military.

The toga was also made of cotton. It was like a long coat and was difficult to make and put on. Rich families had slaves who helped them get dressed. Poor men wore a rough wool cloak. Everybody wore sandals or shoes (called *carbatinae*) made of leather.

FAMILY LIFE

In ancient Rome, families consisted of a father, a mother, single daughters and single sons, often married daughters and married sons, and slaves. In the family, the fathers ruled. At one time, fathers could even decide if a child lived or died. Fathers decided what happened to the family slaves (whether they were bought, sold, freed, or, sometimes, killed). A married son, or a son who was an adult, could not own a house or any property until his father died.

When a child was born, it was taken to the father. If he picked it up, it showed he accepted the child. If he didn't, the child would be sent away and, perhaps, killed. Children were named after they were eight to ten days old.

Children played with toy knights and wheeled horsemen and toy birds and clay dolls.

A Roman reenactor uses a drop spindle to spin yarn for clothes. Her shoes are carbatinae.

GOING TO SCHOOL

Boys and girls started school when they were seven years old. Rich families hired private teachers. These teachers were usually educated slaves. Poor families sent their children to public schools.[3]

Schools had three levels. First, students learned reading and writing and simple math. Just like today, students had to memorize multiplication tables. They often had to say them out loud to the teacher. Second, they learned grammar, history, and Greek and Roman literature. Finally, children had to learn how to speak and think in public. They had debates and gave speeches. The sons of rich families often added to their schooling by going to Athens in Greece or the island of Rhodes to learn from famous philosophers. Poorer boys sometimes hung out with gangs after school. If they got into trouble, they could be required to join the army.

MARRIAGE

Romans married young. Girls could be as young as twelve; boys, fourteen, although they were usually a little older.

There were two kinds of marriages. In the first, the woman still lived with her parents and obeyed only her father. In the second, she lived with her husband and obeyed him.

Marriages were often decided by the father and were based on money or political power. The bride and groom usually didn't have a choice in the matter.

To get engaged, the man gave the woman a coin or an iron ring. At the wedding, the man and woman held hands, agreed to be married, and asked the gods for a blessing. Then the families and guests had a big party. When night came and the first star appeared, the bride left the party and went to her new house. Her husband would be at the doorstep to give her water and fire. These symbolized the elements that were crucial to life through washing and cooking.

A woman could control the family money and property only when her husband died. For this reason, many widows chose not to remarry.

What Were Roman Houses Like?

In ancient Rome, most people were poor. They lived in run-down cottages or rented one-room or two-room apartments in dilapidated buildings called *insulae*. These six-story buildings were built fast and cheap, usually of wood, and weren't safe. When they weren't falling down, they were catching on fire. People stayed there only to sleep. They rarely cooked in their rooms for fear of starting a fire.

The poorer you were, the higher the floor on which you lived. Only the first floor, which was for shops, had running water. People who lived on the higher floors had to carry their water up or pay somebody to carry it up for them. As many as five people slept in a room. There was no plumbing, so people used public bathrooms. The toilets were together in a semicircle so that people could talk to each other while they were there.

Insulae Dianae, built with bricks instead of wood

Rich Romans lived in very nice single-story homes built around a central hall called an atrium. The atrium didn't have a roof, so sunlight and rainwater could come in. Just past the atrium was a second open room called a *peristylium*. It had columns, a garden, and a fountain, and was usually where the owners held parties.

These homes had water brought in through lead pipes (the bigger the pipes, the wealthier the owners). They had their own private bathrooms. Many of these houses didn't have windows because the owners didn't want to look out at the dusty, dirty streets. Their walls were often covered with paintings, many showing realistically drawn animals such as cats, birds, dogs, fish, and peacocks. Some paintings were of snakes, because the Romans thought snakes represented the gods responsible for health and wealth. If the people were really rich, they had mosaics (pictures or designs made out of small stones) on their floors. Many houses had cellars.

The Romans adopted much of their mythology from the Greeks, including the myth of Pegasus. The white flying horse represented immortality to the Romans.

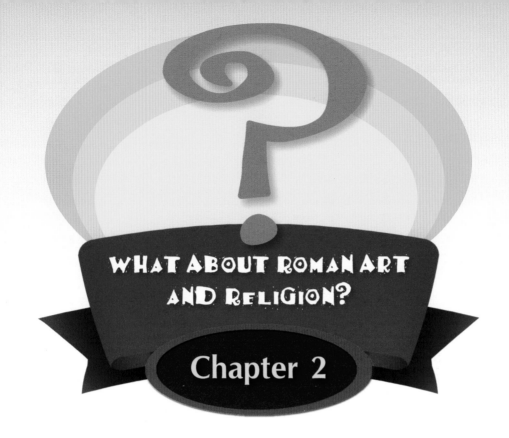

WHAT ABOUT ROMAN ART AND RELIGION?

Chapter 2

As Rome expanded its territory, it brought many well-developed civilizations under its control. After the city's legendary founding in 753 BCE, the Etruscans, the people who ruled central Italy, conquered Rome in 700 BCE. In 509 BCE, however, the Romans regained their independence, and the Roman Republic began. As Rome continued to grow, its people borrowed religious beliefs, art, and architecture from the people they conquered. They were greatly influenced by the Carthaginians and the Greeks, whom they conquered in 146 BCE, after the Third Punic War.

In fact, the Romans shared nearly all the Greek gods. They did change some of the gods' names. For example, the Greek god Zeus, the greatest of all the gods, became the Roman god Jupiter. The Greek god Hermes, the messenger of Zeus, became Mercury. Aphrodite, the Greek goddess of love, became Venus. The Romans believed that gods controlled everything in their lives, so it was important to pray to them all the time. Why did they adopt the gods of other civilizations? When they were trying to conquer their enemies, the Romans believed if they appealed to their enemies' gods, those gods would favor the Romans.

SPQR

This second-century statue of Jupiter, the father of the gods, is at the Louvre in Paris. It had stood in the ancient city of Smyrna (now called Izmir, Turkey).

Three of the most important Roman gods were Jupiter, Mars, and Quirinus. Besides being the greatest god in their pantheon, Jupiter was the god of the sky and the father of the gods, and almost everybody worshiped him. Mars, the god of war, was considered Rome's protector and gave the city its power. Quirinus was the god of the army in times of peace. There were a lot of other gods and goddesses, such as Vesta, the defender of the home; Juno, the goddess of women and childbirth; and Phoebus, the god of light, truth, and music.

Romans believed in a type of heaven called the Elysian Fields. It was like a beautiful sunlit meadow, and getting there wasn't easy. After a person died, his or her soul went to the spirit world. The soul had to get past the unburied dead and go through a disturbing place where people who had been bad in life were being tortured. Then it had to cross five filthy rivers, ferried by Charon, the gods' boat captain. Each soul had to pay Charon a silver coin to be able to ride with him. Thus, the Romans buried their dead with a coin—so that they could pay the ferryman.

Romans often prayed to their deities as a way to get revenge on people. For instance, here's one prayer to Proserpina, the goddess of the underworld: "I beg, pray and beseech you by your majesty to revenge the theft that has been committed against me and to punish whoever has borrowed, stolen or made away with the (items) listed below: six tunics, two cloaks. . . ."[1]

Romans went to temples to pray. These temples were often built for just one god, such as the Temple of Jupiter or the Temple of Apollo. Romans also prayed in their houses. Each home had a small altar and shrine for their household gods, whom they worshiped every day. In fact, praying to household gods was more important than praying to the public ones. Many homes had a *lararium,* a closet built like a small temple in which the household gods, the Lares, were believed to live. The Lares were the guardian spirits of the family. Other gods, called Penates, watched over the food.

Praying to the household gods was so important that even slaves were invited. During family meals, the father, as the head of the family, would pour a drink in honor of these household gods. Sometimes a piece of salt would be thrown onto the fire to thank Vesta for protecting their home.

As the Romans conquered other civilizations, they adopted their religious beliefs and art styles.

Romans also believed in sacrificing animals to please the gods. Certain animals pleased certain gods. Priests sacrificed oxen for Jupiter, sheep for Juno, and horses for Mars. Sacrifices were usually done outside in temple yards. Music was played during the sacrifice to cover the noise.

Romans also worshiped their emperors as if they were gods, starting with Augustus Caesar, who came to power in 27 BCE.

Many Roman artists showed tales from their religion in art. They also portrayed rich people or actual events, such as military victories. Because the Roman Empire was so big and was made of so many different people and regions, Roman art had many styles. The names of most artists have been lost; usually the person who hired the artist was considered more important, so artists' names were not recorded.

Roman sculptors carved life-like statues out of marble.

Early Roman art looked a lot like the art of the Etruscans, and showed the overthrow of Etruscan kings in 509 BCE. Etruscans were famous for making bronze sculptures, and the Romans copied them. They were usually life-sized heroes or important leaders dressed in togas or armor. To make a bronze statue, artists would create the shape they wanted in wax around a clay core. They would cover the wax with more clay, then heat it. The wax would melt and run out, leaving a hollow area between the clay layers. Artists would then pour in molten bronze, which filled the hollow area and took the shape of the statue. When the bronze cooled, the clay was removed, and the bronze statue remained. Even large statues were made this way, although artists had to make them in pieces, then joined the pieces together with molten lead and bronze.

After conquering Greece, which was famous for its marble sculptures, Romans began sculpting from marble as well. Rome got much of its marble from the nearby town of Carrara. Greek statues showed people as they wished they looked. Romans made sculptures of the rich and powerful that showed every wart and blemish. If a person had a crooked nose or double chin, those details were copied exactly on the Roman sculpture.

In the best sculptures, the stone was carved to look like skin. For instance, a sculpture of Caracalla (Marcus Aurelius), the emperor from 211 to 217 CE, shows him with a beard, smooth skin, and real-looking hair. A lot of statues were brightly colored, but experts don't know which colors were used because the colors have worn away over time.

Bronze statue of an aristocratic Roman boy, from the reign of Augustus Caesar, 27 BCE–14 CE

Romans admire a frieze, a carved band of art that runs above doors and windows and below ceilings.

There were two kinds of sculptures—those that showed the whole body, and those that showed just the head (called busts). Many full-sized sculptures were displayed at the Roman Forum and other public buildings.

When making busts of famous people who had died, Romans started with wax death masks that were used during funerals. Those busts were displayed in homes, so the more busts a person had, the more powerful his family was.

Gold coins, which were used from 46 BCE to 96 CE, were made to honor leaders and famous events. Some of those coins have survived, showing people what leaders such as Augustus Caesar looked like.

Emperors liked to have historical scenes painted with them in the action. They often had artists paint gods next to them to show they had divine favor.

Romans also made containers of clay and silver that showed scenes from myths or history. They covered their walls with frescoes, which is painting done on wet plaster. These usually showed adventures of gods, daily life, animals, or landscapes. Mosaics, made from many tiny pieces of glass or stone, and reliefs, which were figures or designs carved out from a flat stone background, were also popular. Most reliefs showed historical events.

The Myth: Romulus and Remus Founded Rome

The ancient Romans believed that Rome was founded in 753 BCE by twins Romulus and Remus. They were the sons of the god Mars and a Vestal Virgin (a priestess). Years before they were born, Aeneas, a warrior who fought in the Trojan War, settled in Italy and founded the city of Lavinium. One of his descendants, Numitor, became king of Alba Longa. But Numitor's brother, Amulius, wanted to be king, so he threw his brother in jail and took over. He also forced Numitor's daughter, Rhea Silvia, to become a priestess so that she wouldn't marry and have children who could one day try to take over his kingdom. Mars interfered with his plans and met with Rhea Silvia, who gave birth to Romulus and Remus.

As babies, they were tossed into the Tiber River by their evil uncle Amulius. They were saved by a she-wolf, who nursed them until Faustulus, a kind shepherd, came along to raise them.

Romulus and Remus, *the founders of Rome, painted by Peter Paul Rubens, 1614–1616*

The boys grew up to be mighty warriors. They learned the truth about their family, then defeated Amulius and freed Numitor. They decided to start their own city, and chose the place by the Tiber River where they had been saved by the she-wolf. The place had seven hills. The brothers could not decide which one of them should rule, so they asked the gods for a sign.

Remus saw the first sign—six vultures flying over Aventine Hill. Then Romulus saw a sign—twelve vultures flying over Palatine Hill. The brothers got into a fight when Remus made fun of Romulus, and Romulus killed Remus. Romulus became king of the city named after him, Rome. He ruled for a long time before, according to legend, he was taken into heaven and made a god. Romulus was the first of seven mythical kings who ruled early Rome. The others were Numa Pompilius, Tullus Hostilius, Ancus Martius, Tarquinius Priscus, Servius Tullius, and Tarquinius Superbus.

A slave serves wine at a feast enjoyed by the Roman nobility.

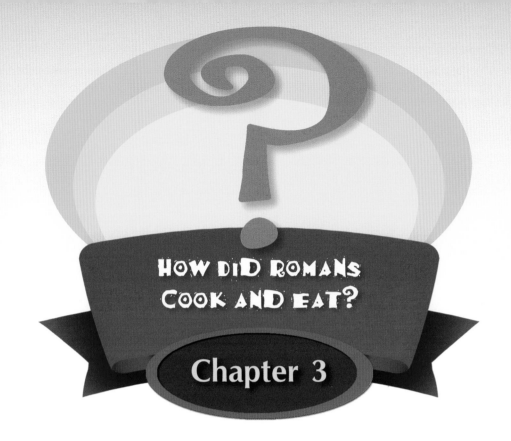

HOW DID ROMANS COOK AND EAT?

Chapter 3

Marcus Gavius Apicius, who lived in the first century CE, was one of the most famous cooks in ancient Rome. He reputedly spent a vast fortune seeking and preparing rare foods. One of his favorite foods, according to Roman biographer Pliny, was flamingo tongues. About three hundred years after Apicius' death, around 450 of his recipes were compiled in a cookbook called *On Cookery*. These recipes have influenced European cooking ever since.

What did Romans eat? They liked to eat birds, so they raised and ate pigeons (squab, a delicacy, is a baby pigeon). Sometimes they sacrificed pigeons to the gods. Flamingo was served especially during banquets. Some of those banquets, which could last 10 hours, were so big and varied, they included platters of giraffe, ostrich, wild boar, and lion. Another delicacy was roasted dormouse. Most of these animals were killed during the daily public games.

Romans ate three meals a day, but not like we do. They had two breakfasts and one dinner. Why not call the second breakfast lunch? That's one of the great mysteries of the ancient world.[1]

The first breakfast was usually cheese, fruit, bread, and milk or wine. (The Romans drank wine mixed with water; the water weakened the wine, and the alcohol in the wine made the water safe to drink.) The second breakfast wasn't actually served like a meal. Basically, Romans snacked on leftovers from the previous day's dinner. There might be meat, fruit, fish, cheese, and more wine.

The big meal was dinner, called *cena,* which was served late in the afternoon. The entire family, which might not be together for breakfast, ate dinner together. This meal consisted of *gustatio,* which were like hors d'oeuvres (finger food); *prima mensa* ("first table," or main course); and *secunda mensa* ("second table," or dessert). Although their desserts did not contain sugar, the Romans sweetened their foods with honey or syrup made from grape juice.

Roman-style bread

SPQR

An olive press from Pompeii. Olives were served whole or as relish, or they were pressed for their oil. Olive oil was used in foods, in lamps, and in place of soap.

Wealthy Romans gossip over grapes.

Wealthy Romans loved to have dinner parties. Some were small; others were huge affairs that often featured entertainers. They didn't dine from chairs or high tables like we do today, but ate while lying on couches or soft cushions. Sitting up to eat was considered rude.[2] Slaves served meat (usually pork, lamb, rabbit, or chicken), fish, vegetables, snacks, fresh or dried fruit, and, once again, wine. Bread was served, and olive oil in which to dunk it. Romans also ate a hot wheat porridge called *puls*.

Poor people ate a lot of the free bread that was passed out daily by Roman leaders. Grain for the bread came from Egypt. A favorite dish was a stew made of wheat, barley, and beans. Common people also ate *puls*, grain, and olives, and, of course, they drank wine.

All Romans ate with their fingers—except for soup, for which they used a spoon. They didn't use forks, although they did use knives to cut bread and meat. (Slaves cut the food for rich Romans.) When they were finished, they'd just dump their plates on the floor. Slaves cleaned up the mess.

SPQR

A brick oven from Pompeii. Similar ovens are still used in bakeries and restaurants that serve pizza.

How did Romans cook their food? The poor rarely cooked at home because of the risk of fire. Instead, they went to street vendors to buy food. If they couldn't afford that, they'd eat the free bread. Sometimes they would bring wheat to a local baker and have him make fresh bread for them. This bread was very coarse, and it often included plenty of grit that would wear down their teeth.

Slaves or professional cooks made meals for wealthy Romans. Brick ovens were used for baking or roasting. A cook would light a wood fire near the side of the oven. When the wood had burned to hot coals, the bricks would be hot enough to bake bread or roast meat.

When Romans didn't want to cook, they ate out. They could go to a little street restaurant called a *thermopolium,* which sold warmed wine and the ancient equivalent of fast food, such as hot sausages, cheese, and dates. There were also plenty of hot food shops and bars (called *tabernae*). In fact, there were thousands of such food shops in Rome. Romans could also find restaurants at the public baths.

Roman Food Ingredients

Ancient Romans liked extra flavor in their food, so they would add spices and herbs to it. They often used spices found in the places they conquered, such as pepper from India. One of the Roman spices was a violet or white flowering plant called *saturei*, which was used with beans. *Levisticum officinale* is a plant with yellow flowers; the Romans used its dried roots as a spice.

They also flavored their foods with sauces made from such ingredients as figs, mint, and fish guts. Depending on the type of fish used, these fish sauces were called *liquamen* or *muria* and were used instead of salt. A spicy fish sauce called *garum* was made from the blood and guts of mackerel, mullet, or other strong-flavored fish.[3] A sweet sauce called *passum* was made from boiling new wine or grape juice.

If Romans wanted a taste of fig, they could go to the nearest fig tree and take some of its fruit. They'd boil the figs until their juice thickened into a kind of syrup. Sometimes they would feed figs to their pigs; the figs would sweeten the animal's liver—flavoring the meat before slaughter. For a minty flavor, they used pennyroyal (*Mentha pulegium,* or *poleiminze*), which grew in flooded areas.

Silphium, which has a very strong taste and smell, was used in place of onions and garlic, but they'd only use a little because of how strong it was. Nevertheless, they used so much of it, the plant became extinct in Rome.[4]

Romans used figs to flavor their foods.

A reenactor shows the perils of chariot racing.

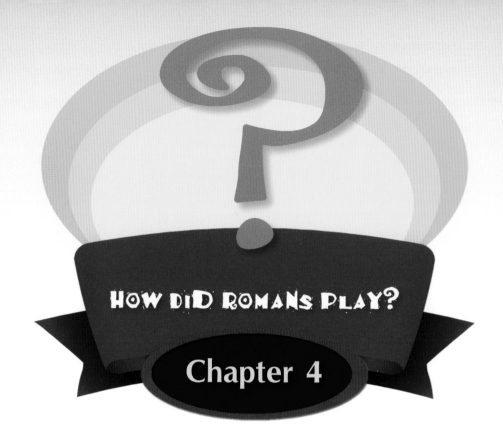

HOW DID ROMANS PLAY?

Chapter 4

In Rome, fun often happened on a plain near the Tiber River called the Campus Martius (Field of Mars). At one time it had been a marsh, then a field where soldiers drilled and practiced for war. Before it was completely developed with houses, Romans turned the campus into a combination of a playground and a track and field.

Ancient Romans didn't have sports as we know them. They weren't interested in running or throwing or jumping like the ancient Greeks did. They also didn't like Greek boxing, maybe because it wasn't rough enough. Greek boxers covered their knuckles with leather thongs, sort of a smaller version of boxing gloves, and then hit each other. Roman boxers wore gloves that were studded with metal spikes, making the fights much bloodier and more dangerous.

Romans liked to watch chariot races and gladiator fights, but they liked to play Roman ball—one of the few games that didn't involve swords or metal-studded boxing gloves. They played it on a field. Most of the players gathered in a circle in the middle of the field. Players outside the circle would throw a ball at them. If the thrower missed, he got a point. Whoever had the fewest points at the end would win.[1]

Romans also played a version of soccer, although it was played in the streets and there weren't any goals. There was also a game that legionnaires played to prepare for combat. It was like a combination of today's soccer, rugby, and mixed martial arts and was very rough. Today it's called *calcio fiorentino*.

Romans liked board games that we still play today. For instance, they played Roman checkers (you had to get five stones in a row on the board to win), chess, backgammon, and tic-tac-toe.

They played a game called knucklebones, or *astragali,* which used the small anklebones of sheep. The bones had six sides, and players tossed them into the air and tried to catch them on the back of their hands. They could also be played like dice, with each side having a different number value, such as 3 or 4 or 6. Some knucklebones were made of marble, silver, or precious stones.

Many Romans liked to gamble and would bet on just about everything—board games, dice games, war games, gladiator fights, chariot races, horse races, you name it.

CHARIOT RACES

Roman chariot races were also dangerous and scary because the chariots—as many as twelve at a time—went extremely fast around a track of sand that had very tight corners. The chariots would bang and bounce and crash, and sometimes a charioteer would die. Drivers could be knocked off their chariots and run over by other horses or chariots.

Bone die and knucklebones

Lots of Roman towns had racetracks, but Rome had the biggest with the Circus Maximus. The "circus" was a circle or a track for racing. The Circus Maximus was 1,870 feet long and 460 feet wide—the largest in the empire. The stands reached as high as 92 feet and could hold as many as 380,000 spectators. In the center was a barrier called the *spina.* It featured large trophies, statues, a lap counter, and an Egyptian obelisk.

There were as many as twenty-four chariot races in a day. Each race consisted of one warm-up lap and then seven official laps. The first one to finish the seven laps was the winner. A group of judges on a platform halfway down the side of the track made sure every driver followed the rules. If they didn't, they'd be disqualified. The winner received money, a gold necklace, and a palm leaf.

Chariot races were considered family entertainment, so children were allowed to attend. Because of that, men and women could sit together (they couldn't at the Colosseum during gladiator fights). People arrived early to get good seats. There were places to buy food (a kind of donut was very popular) and drinks.

There were four teams divided into colors—red, white, blue, and green. Drivers would wear their colors on their helmets and sleeveless tunics. People would bet on which team they thought would win.

The Circus Maximus

Before the races, there was a parade that would include athletes, race officials, priests, musicians, jesters, and acrobats. The chariot teams, which had been hidden from view, then drove onto the track to the cheers of the crowd. Once they had positioned themselves behind the starting line, a trumpet would sound, and silence would fall over the stadium. A race official would raise a white cloth. When the cloth was dropped, the race began, although on that first lap, no passing was allowed. After that, it was every driver for himself. The action was fast and furious. Trumpets blared when the winner crossed the finish line. People cheered. Money from bets was made and lost.

And then the crowd would wait for the next race.

THEATER

While the Romans didn't have TV or movies, they did have the theater. They enjoyed comedies, sad plays called tragedies, and plays called pantomimes in which a single actor called a mime didn't speak but used motions and gestures to tell the story. Some of these plays were violent, others were just not suitable for children. Plays were held in theaters, which were smaller and more comfortable than large amphitheaters that held gladiator fights and wild beast shows.

Pantomimes were very popular because they showed everyday life. Comedies were also popular, especially ones that used jokes that mentioned current people or events, or even said mean things about the gods. Many had a lot of horseplay and rough action. That was fine with the audience, which was usually loud and fun-loving. People cheered and laughed and clapped and made sure the actors knew they were there.

Most actors were slaves or freed slaves. They usually wore masks, and the masks showed what they were feeling or something about their personality. There were masks that showed anger, fear, sadness, happiness, and excitement. Plays could be told by dancing mimes—the best dancers became very famous—or by just one actor who played different parts by wearing different masks.

Not many Romans wrote plays. Instead, they performed a lot of Greek plays. Sometimes they changed them a little to be closer to Roman culture. Many of the plays involved myths (like Romulus and Remus and the founding of Rome) or history (such as how Rome beat Carthage, and General Hannibal).

If you didn't like the play, you could always watch the dancing girls, jugglers, and tightrope walkers who were also part of the show.

Romans attending the theater

Roman Health

Medicine was important in ancient Rome to keep soldiers and gladiators fighting as well as to keep people healthy.

Romans understood the importance of clean water. Julius Caesar was one of the first generals who emphasized building forts away from insect-infested swamps. He once had a swamp drained and a forest planted. Doctors had drains and sewers built to get sewage (dirty water) away from troops.[2]

Before Caesar's reign there were no true doctors in Rome. It was up to the head of the household to take care of the family by using herbs and praying to the gods. Romans believed that the best thing you could do was keep fit. They'd rather spend money on staying in shape than on doctors. But Romans learned the advantage of having doctors from the Greeks.

Emperor Augustus realized the key to the

A doctor removes an arrowhead from the leg of a wounded legionnaire.

empire was good doctors and medicine. Doctors were trained in schools (doctors kept records of what worked and what didn't in battle) and hospitals were built. Medicine became very advanced, and in fact Roman medical practices were the most sophisticated in the world until the nineteenth and twentieth centuries.

Doctors used such medical tools as forceps (an instrument used to grab objects), scalpels (a surgical knife), catheters (a slender tube), and even arrow extractors. While they didn't understand what germs were, they did understand to keep their instruments clean. They boiled them after each use, and they tried not to use the same ones on different patients. They also practiced good hygiene; their regular bathing helped combat germs.

During surgery, they used painkillers derived from opium poppies and special seeds called henbane seeds. Wounds were washed in acetum (vinegar acid), which was a better antiseptic than what was used in nineteenth-century Europe.

Ancient doctors knew that arteries and veins carried blood. They knew how to use tourniquets to stop blood flow. They used amputation to prevent deadly gangrene.

Much of this knowledge was lost after the Roman Empire fell in 476 CE. It wasn't relearned until 1,300 years later.

A life-size bronze statue of a resting Roman gladiator at the Museo Nazionale Romano in Palazzo Massimo

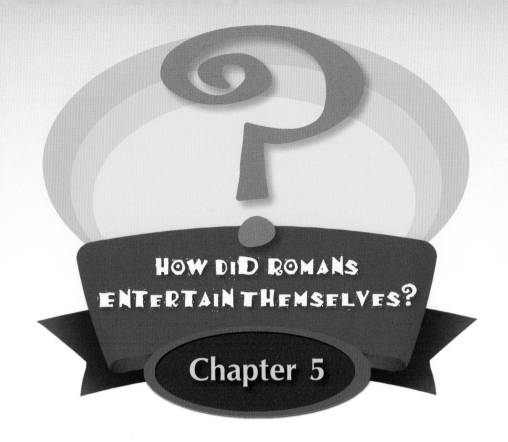

HOW DID ROMANS ENTERTAIN THEMSELVES?

Chapter 5

Some of the most popular spectator sports in ancient Rome were the gladiator fights. Gladiators were named after a Roman sword called the *gladius*. They were usually criminals sentenced to death, prisoners of war, or slaves. As a result, people didn't think much of them—at least until they saw how well the gladiators fought in the arena.

Sometimes free men—even rich free men—volunteered because they wanted money and fame and excitement. Gladiators sometimes got all three if they were very good, but even then it was a hard and dangerous life. A few women competed, but most Romans didn't approve of that.[1]

Gladiators had to swear an oath that said, "I will endure to be burned, to be bound, to be beaten and to be killed by the sword."[2] They were taught how to die: without begging for their lives or yelling. They had to accept death with courage. Many were badly injured or even killed—either by other gladiators or by wild animals such as lions, bears, bulls, tigers, elephants, rhinoceroses, or alligators that were let into the ring. Even ostriches were used in fights—and if you think fighting them was easy, you haven't seen ostriches lash out with their sharp two-toed feet.

In fact, animals were used in fights before people were (as many as 5,000 animals were killed in one day). Animals were abused to make them mean and more ready to fight, actions that today would send their owners to jail. If a gladiator was devoured (that rarely happened), the crowd would cheer. Romans were a tough crowd.

The best gladiators were as popular as today's famous athletes. If they kept winning, they could get rich and be treated like heroes or movie stars. One gladiator won 53 fights. Another won more than 20 fights. Gladiators were often very popular with young girls. Here's an example of graffiti that was written on walls: "Thrax is the heart-throb of all the girls."[3]

Sometimes, a gladiator would do so well he would win a wooden sword, called a *rudius*—and his freedom. Free gladiators could continue to fight for money, but they often became trainers in gladiator schools or bodyguards for wealthy people.

New gladiators had to go to gladiator school, called a *ludus*. Schools were usually found near the stadiums where gladiators fought. For instance, the largest school in the empire, the Ludus Magnus, was located next to the Colosseum in Rome. It included a practice arena that still exists as a ruin.

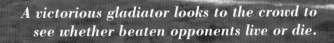

*A victorious gladiator looks to the crowd to
see whether beaten opponents live or die.*

Many of the gladiator schools were former prisons. They were usually cold and dark, with no comfortable furniture—sometimes no furniture at all. Gladiators lived in rows of cells without windows or views of the outside. One school at Pompeii had ceilings so low, gladiators could only sit or lie down.

Gladiator training was long, hard, and expensive. New gladiators were given a wooden sword to train with because officials didn't want them hurting or killing themselves by practicing with a real sword. They also didn't want gladiators attacking their trainers and escaping. Romans remembered what happened when the gladiator Spartacus escaped in 73 BCE. He formed an army with other escaped gladiators, and they terrorized the countryside for two years before they were all captured and killed.

Gladiator trainers got help from special instructors known as *doctores.* These were specialists in a specific weapon or style of fighting. For instance, gladiators used a curved Thracian short sword called a *sica,* lance, or a net and a trident. They practiced footwork. They learned how to parry (dodge or avoid a sword) and feint (fake a sword thrust). They attacked a six-foot wooden pole, called a *palus,* and sparred with others. They trained long hours because, like today's pro athletes, it was their job.

Gladiators would enter the arena to a huge roar from the crowd. Spectators were excited about the   upcoming show. This was reality entertainment at its bloodiest, and people bet on who they thought would win and lose. The gladiators would gather in front of the emperor if he was there, or the games sponsor (the *munerarius*). Many experts believed gladiators would say, "We who are about

Sica sword

The Roman Colosseum, which still
stands and is open to tourists, was the
site of the biggest and best gladiator and
animal fights.

to die salute you!" Others aren't so sure, claiming there is no evidence
to support that they did.[4]

Gladiators were matched against each other based on experience and
ability. Nobody wanted to see a talent mismatch, and no gladiator wanted
to fight in one. The fight was about pride and glory as much as victory.
Beating an inferior opponent brought no glory. Good competition also
made for more interesting betting.

Gladiators won by killing an opponent, wounding him, or stripping
him of his weapons. Many of the fights ended in draws. While the emperor or *munerarius* could decide a fallen fighter's fate, few fights ended
in death, in part because it was so expensive to train gladiators.

When a gladiator was wounded and wanted to quit, he would hold
up an index finger. That's when the crowd would decide whether or not
they wanted him to live or die. Some believe that the crowd, and then
the emperor, would give a thumbs up to die or a thumbs down to live,

but there also is no specific evidence for this. The written record includes the phrase *pollicem premere* (to press the thumb) to live, which might mean those who wanted the gladiator to live kept their thumbs pressed against their hands, while those who wanted death waved their thumbs in any direction. The final say went to the emperor or games sponsor.

If a gladiator was killed, a man dressed as Charon—the ferryman who sailed the dead to Pluto's realm in the underworld—checked to make sure the gladiator was dead. Then a slave would drag the body through a gate called the *Porta Libitinensis* (Libitina was the goddess of death, corpses, and funerals, so this was her gate).

And then the next fight would begin.

Reenactors demonstrate gladiator training.

Gladiators

There were many kinds of gladiators. Each had a specific role, wore specific outfits, and used specific weapons.

THRACIAN: They used the Thracian sword as well as a small round shield called a parma. They wore a wide-brimmed crested helmet with a front piece called a visor.

SECUTOR and SAMNITE: They were both heavily armed, used a sword or a lance, and carried a rectangular shield much like Roman legionnaires used. They wore an egg-shaped metal helmet and had armor on their right arms and left legs.

MURMILLO: They were less armed than Secutors. They wore helmets decorated with fish.

RETIARIUS: They were the only gladiators whose heads and faces were unprotected. In fact, the only armor they had just protected their arms. They fought with a net and a trident, and sometimes a small dagger. They were the most mobile gladiators, but also the ones most likely to be killed or seriously wounded.

BESTIARIUS: These gladiators trained and fought animals. They were the least popular gladiators and rarely became famous or rich. They usually were armed with whips and spears and didn't have much armor—or much of a chance for survival.

Different types of gladiators fought each other, such as a Thracian facing a Murmillo or a Secutor going against a Retiarius. That created weapon mismatches, but it also added to the excitement—something the Romans craved.[5]

Gladiators left to right:
Thracian, Secutor, Samnite, Murmillo, Retiarus

Parts of the Roman Forum have survived from antiquity. The Forum was the center of city life.

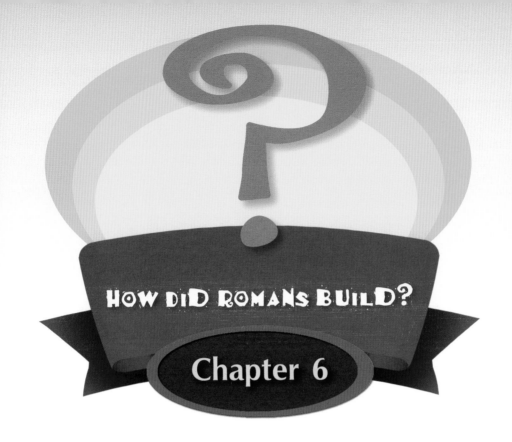

HOW DID ROMANS BUILD?

Chapter 6

Romans loved to build and build big. Whether the current project was the Colosseum, the Circus Maximus, the Pantheon, or sewers and public baths, builders never got much rest.

Romans liked to borrow building designs. From the Etruscans they took arches, from the Greeks they had classical columns. They later developed the vault (a big room that didn't need inside columns for support) and the dome.

What did they build with? From nearby quarries they dug travertine, which was a kind of limestone. Roman soil was rich in volcanic sand called pozzolana. Builders mixed that with lime and water to make cement. Later, they added other materials such as gravel and tiny stones to make concrete, which was perfect for building.

Most buildings were made of concrete, with brick on the outside. Bricks were made from clay and needed two years to dry. Builders also used tufa rock, which was cut from quarries in the summer and left out in the air for two years to harden. They learned how to cast bronze and bake terra-cotta (a hard clay).

Building took a lot of planning. It also took a lot of workers, and these were mostly slaves.

Roman architecture peaked during the empire. One of the most famous Roman buildings was the Pantheon, an ancient temple to the Roman gods that still stands in near perfect condition. It was first built in 27 BCE by Marcus Agrippa for his father-in-law, the Emperor Augustus. It was destroyed by a fire in 80 CE and rebuilt by the Emperor Domitian. In 110 CE it was hit by lightning and burned again. The Emperor Hadrian tried again around 125 CE, this time using a different design and materials that were less likely to burn, such as marble and concrete. Hadrian honored Agrippa by putting a saying on the front that reads, *M. Agrippa cos tertium fecit* (M Agrippa made this).[1] In 608 CE it was given to Pope Boniface IV and was converted into a Christian church.

The Pantheon's walls are 20 feet thick. Its built-in arches were made to handle the weight of the heavy domed roof, which is 142 feet high and 142 feet wide. It has a 27-foot hole in the center called an oculus to let in air and light. It also lets in rain, which in Roman times was captured below and used for drinking water.

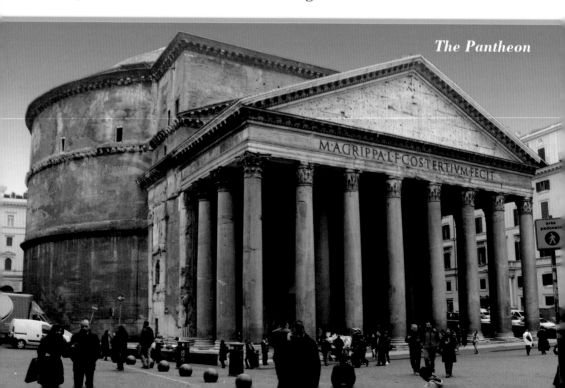

The Pantheon

The cell in Mamertine Prison where St. Peter was said to be jailed. The hole in the ceiling is where prisoners were dropped. The altar honors St. Peter— the upside-down cross represents St. Peter's upside-down crucifixion.

How was the dome built? Workers started with a wooden mold, then they covered it with concrete. As they moved toward the top of the dome, they used lighter concrete. At the very top they mixed in volcanic pumice, one of the lightest stones in existence.

Another famous building was the Mamertine Prison. Legend says that St. Peter was jailed there for a while. Prisoners were dropped into the prison through a hole in the floor. The only exit, so the saying went, was by death.

Roman builders didn't let poor ground or climate conditions slow them down. For instance, in the seventh century BCE, they wanted to build a market on an old cemetery in a wet, muddy marsh and shallow lake. Builders drained the lake and marsh, moved the graves, and started building what became the Forum Romanum (Roman Forum).

The Forum was a huge place where people could shop and worship and socialize. It had stores and temples and even a senate house and law courts. It was Rome's business heart, and ruins of the place still stand. It even had what was called the "golden milestone." The distances on every road from Rome were measured by it.

The Forum was destroyed during the Middle Ages. Scientists began digging it out in 1803. The Forum doesn't look as impressive now as it did during Roman times, but there are plenty of ruins to explore.

The Forum was built next to Palatine Hill, where the emperors and other wealthy people lived. Many had very big, very nice houses. In fact, we get the word *palace* from the houses on Palatine Hill.

To get water to the cities, builders constructed aqueducts. Basically these were arched bridges that carried water from a large body of water, such as a lake, to a city. They worked using gravity—the water started from a spring in the hills and was collected in a reservoir (a man-made lake) to build pressure and make sure there was a steady water flow to lower ground. Some aqueducts were more than 50 miles long.

Aqueducts had three channels or pipes through which water could flow. If there wasn't much water, it would just flow through the middle channel to go to public fountains. If there was more water, it went through the middle and one side channel and for fountains and public baths. If there was a lot of water, it went to fountains, baths, and homes.

Aqueducts were supported by rounded Roman arches. Romans got the arch idea from the Etruscans.

Roman Roads

The Appian Way

Without good roads, the Roman Empire might never have existed. Why is that? Because the Romans needed to move their armies all over the empire in times of war, and for an empire as large as Rome's (which covered Europe and North Africa from Spain to the Middle East), good roads were crucial. Builders made sure that the roads could handle heavy loads such as big pieces of military equipment or wagons full of supplies.

Builders designed their roads based on the kind of conditions they had. For instance, in North Africa, which was hot and dry with lots of desert, a gravel road worked best. In wet places, arching roads were built, with the center higher than the sides. This would let rain run off into ditches.

After soldiers dug out the road's path, builders would make a foundation of tightly packed layers. First they'd put down sand and roll it flat. Then they'd use small stones and roll that flat. Then they'd use large stones called gravel and roll that flat. Finally, they'd put paving stones on top.

Probably the most famous of all Roman roads was the 350-mile Appian Way, which was named for its builder, Roman consul Appius Claudius Caecus. It was built in 312 BCE and linked Rome with the Italian towns of Capua and Brindisi. Parts of the road still exist.

Roads were also used by travelers, merchants, and traders. They brought goods and food from places such as Egypt and even India.

MAKE A ROMAN MOSAIC

To make mosaics, artists would take small pieces of stone, glass, tile, and other hard material to form a picture. Each of these pieces was one-third to one-half inch across, and they came in many colors, including red, brown, green, and white. Each piece was pressed into clay or cement. The number of pieces used depended on the size of the mosaic, but it could be in the thousands.

Mosaics often showed scenes of history and everyday life. Some were of standard designs, such as a gladiator, bird, or seahorse. Wealthy Romans could get more personalized designs that reflected themselves or their families. At first, mosaics were used just for floors in homes and buildings. Later, they were also used for walls. You can make a simple mosaic with lots of little squares of colored paper glued to a piece of cardboard. Or you could use black and white pebbles, which you can buy at any gardening store, and set them in plaster of paris or clay.

If you use paper, make sure to have different shades of the same colors, such as light red and dark red, and light blue and dark blue, and so on. The pieces should be about 1/4 inch (1/2 cm) square. To get a design idea, look at several pictures of mosaics—or of anything else you'd like to show in your mosaic.

BCE

753	According to legend, Romulus and Remus found Rome.
700	Etruscans conquer Rome.
509	Etruscans are kicked out and the Roman Republic begins.
264–241	First Punic War against Carthage: Rome wins.
218–201	Second Punic War against Carthage: Rome beats Hannibal, winning again.
149–146	Third Punic War against Carthage: Rome destroys Carthage; Greece becomes a province of Rome.
73–71	Gladiator Spartacus leads a slave revolt.
60	Rome is ruled by Julius Caesar, Crassus, and Pompey; the three are called the Triumvirate.
57	Julius Caesar conquers Gaul.
53	In Rome's first war against Persia, Crassus is defeated.
49	Julius Caesar crosses Rubicon River and takes Rome.
47	Julius Caesar invades Egypt; he falls in love with Egypt's queen Cleopatra.
44	Julius Caesar becomes dictator for life; a month later, in March, he is killed by Brutus and Cassius.
43	Mark Antony, Octavian, and Lepidus form the Second Triumvirate.
37	Mark Antony marries Cleopatra.

| 27 | After a long civil war, Octavian changes his name to Augustus Caesar and becomes the first Roman Emperor. He rules for 41 years (until 14 CE). |

CE

25	Agrippa builds the Pantheon.
64	Fire during Emperor Nero's rule destroys much of the city.
79	Mount Vesuvius erupts, burying Pompeii, Herculaneum, and Stabiae in volcanic ash.
118–128	Emperor Hadrian rebuilds Pantheon.
217	The Baths of Caracalla open.
284	The Roman Empire is divided into East and West.
306	Constantine I becomes the first Christian emperor of Rome; he will reign over both East and West until 337.
410	Rome is sacked by Goths.
455	Rome is sacked by Vandals.
476	Fall of the Western Roman Empire; the Eastern Roman Empire will last for about another thousand years.

The Colosseum is visible behind the ruins of the Roman Forum. To the right is Palatine Hill.

Introduction. Establishing an Empire

1. Nigel Rodgers, *Ancient Rome* (London, Hermes House, 2006), p. 154.
2. Time-Life Editors, *Empires Ascendant–TimeFrame 400 BCE-CE 200*, (Alexandria, Va.: Time-Life Books, 1987), pp. 57–58.
3. Rodgers, p. 184.
4. Ibid., pp. 206–207.

Chapter 1. How Did Romans Live Their Daily Lives?

1. Time-Life Editors, *Empires Ascendant–TimeFrame 400 BCE-CE 200,* (Alexandria, Va.: Time-Life Books, 1987), pp. 45–47.
2. Ibid., p. 99
3. *Daily Life in Ancient Rome,* http://www.ancient-rome.biz/daily-life.html
4. Joan Liversidge, *Everyday Life in the Roman Empire* (New York: G.P. Putnam's Sons, 1976), p. 183.

Chapter 2. What About Roman Art and Religion?

1. Joan Liversidge, *Everyday Life in the Roman Empire* (New York: G.P. Putnam's Sons, 1976), p. 182.
2. *Romulus and Remus: The Beginning of Rome,* http://www.ancient-rome.biz/remus-romulus.html

Chapter 3. How Did Romans Cook and Eat?

1. *Daily Life in Ancient Rome,* http://www.ancient-rome.biz/daily-life.html
2. University of Vermont: *Daily Life in Rome* (Food)

http://www.uvm.edu/~classics/webresources/life/food.html
3. Sally Grainger, "Garum/Liquamen," http://www.geocities.com/Athens/Ithaca/8337/c_garum.html
4. Cathy K. Kaufman, *Cooking in Ancient Civilizations* (Westport, Conn.: Greenwood Press, 2006), p. 111.

Chapter 4. How Did Romans Play?

1. Jake Halpern, "Balls and Blood," *Sports Illustrated,* August 4, 2008, pp. 42–44.
2. Chris Trueman, *Ancient Roman Medicine,* http://www.historylearningsite.co.uk/medicine_in_ancient_rome.htm

Chapter 5. How Did Romans Entertain Themselves?

1. Barbara F. McManus, *Gladiators,* http://www.vroma.org/~bmcmanus/arena.html
2. Ibid.
3. Ibid.
4. Ibid.
5. Barbara F. McManus, The College of New Rochelle, http://www.vroma.org/~bmcmanus/arena.html

Chapter 6. How Did Romans Build?

1. Reid Bramblett and Jeffrey Kennedy, *Top 10 Rome–Your Guide To The 10 Best of Everything* (London: Sargasso Media, 2002), pp. 14–15

Books

Adams, Simon. *Life in Ancient Rome.* Boston, MA: Kingfisher Publications, 2005.

Honan, Linda, and Ellen Kosmer. *Spend the Day in Ancient Rome: Projects and Activities That Bring the Past to Life.* Hoboken, NJ: J. Wiley & Sons, 1998.

James, Simon. *Ancient Rome.* New York: DK Publishing, 2004.

Morris, Ting. *Arts and Crafts of Ancient Rome.* North Mankato, MN: Smart Apple Media, 2007.

Nardo, Don. *Games of Ancient Rome.* San Diego, CA: Lucent Books Inc., 2000.

Rome. London: Dorling Kindersley Limited, 2006.

Waryncia, Lou, and Kenneth Sheldon. *If I Were a Kid in Ancient Rome.* Chicago: Cricket Books, 2007.

Works Consulted

Bramblett, Reid, and Jeffrey Kennedy. *Top 10 Rome–Your Guide to the 10 Best of Everything.* London: Sargasso Media, 2002.

Cullen, John. *A Walk in Ancient Rome.* New York: Simon & Schuster, 2005.

Freeman, Charles. *Egypt, Greece & Rome.* Oxford, NY: Oxford University Press, 2004.

Halpern, Jake. "Balls and Blood," *Sports Illustrated,* August 4, 2008, pp. 42–44.

Kaufman, Cathy K. *Cooking in Ancient Civilizations.* Westport, CT: Greenwood Press, 2006.

Liversidge, Joan. *Everyday Life in the Roman Empire.* London & New York: B.T. Batsford LTD & G.P. Putnam's Sons, 1976.

MacDougall, Patrick Leonard. *The Campaigns of Hannibal.* Yardley, PA: Westholme Publishing, 2007. Originally published 1858 by Longman, Brown, Green, Longmans & Roberts.

MacKay, Christopher S. *Ancient Rome.* New York: Cambridge University Press, 2004.

McManus, Barbara F. *Arena: Gladiatorial Games.* The College of New Rochelle http://www.vroma.org/~bmcmanus/arena.html

Meijer, Fik. *The Gladiator.* New York: Thomas Dunne Books, St. Martin's Press, 2003.

Pescarin, Sofia. *Rome: A Guide to the Eternal City.* Vercelli, Italy: White Star S.r.l., Barnes & Noble, 2000.

Rodgers, Nigel. *Ancient Rome.* London: Hermes House, 2006.

Time-Life Editors. *Empires Ascendant: TimeFrame 400 BCE-CE 200.* Alexandria, VA: Time-Life Books, 1987.

Trueman, Chris. *Ancient Roman Medicine.* http://www.historylearningsite.co.uk/medicine_in_ancient_rome.htm

FURTHER READING

On the Internet

Ancient Rome
http://www.ancient-rome.biz/

Grout, James. Encyclopaedia Romana: "The Roman Gladiator," University of Chicago.
http://penelope.uchicago.edu/~grout/encyclopaedia_romana/gladiators/gladiators.html

Lendering, Jona. "Hannibal," Livius.org.
http://www.livius.org/ha-hd/hannibal/hannibal.html

Metropolitan Museum of Art: Greek and Roman Art
http://www.metmuseum.org/Works_of_Art/greek_and_roman_art

Powers, Jennifer Goodall. *Ancient Weddings,* 1997
http://ablemedia.com/ctcweb/consortium/ancientweddings7.html

Roman Mosaics
http://www.bbc.co.uk/history/ancient/romans/mosaics_gallery.shtml

Roman Weddings
http://www.unrv.com/culture/roman-weddings.php

University of Vermont: Daily Life in Rome (Food)
http://www.uvm.edu/~classics/webresources/life/food.html

align (ah-LYN)—To join with others.

aqueduct (AA-kwih-dukt)—A bridge-like structure that uses gravity to carry water from a pond or reservoir to a town.

atrium (AY-tree-um)—A large, open room within a building or house.

cavalry (KAA-vul-ree)—Horse-riding soldiers.

Elysian Fields (ee-LEE-jun FEELDS)—The ancient Romans' version of heaven; a beautiful meadow were the dead would go if they had been good in life.

Etruscans (ee-TRUS-kins)—Ancient people who ruled central Italy before Rome became a power.

fresco (FRES-koh)—A painting done on wet plaster walls; the paint would dry in the plaster.

gangrene (GANG-green)—Death and decay of body tissue on a living person.

Gaul (GALL)—An area in what is now France.

hors d'oeuvres (or DERVS)—Finger food, usually served before a meal.

insulae (IN-suh-lee)—Roman apartment buildings.

legionnaire (lee-jun-AYR)—A Roman foot soldier.

mercenary (MER-suh-nay-ree)—A soldier who is paid to fight for a country other than his own.

Middle Ages—A period of European history from the fall of Rome (476 CE) to the beginning of the Italian Renaissance (around 1500 CE).

mosaic (moh-ZAY-ik)—A picture or design made of small stones or pieces of glass placed in clay, tile, or mortar.

obelisk (AH-buh-lisk)—A tall, four-sided shaft of stone with the top shaped like a pyramid.

oculus (OK-yoo-lus)—A hole in a dome, such as the hole in the dome of the Pantheon.

Punic (PYOO-nik) **Wars**—Three wars fought between Rome and Carthage. Rome won all three and finally destroyed Carthage.

Pyrrhic (PEER-ik) **victory**—A victory that is more costly that it was worth.

tourniquet (TUR-nih-ket)—A band of cloth or leather that is tied around a wound to temporarily stop the flow of blood.